D1189957

INGEBORG'S ISLE ROYALE

by Ingeborg Holte

edited by Jane Lind

Ingeborg Holte

Women's Times Publishing

Grand Marais, Minnesota 55604

CREDITS:
Thanks to the following for permission to reprint photographs: Tim Cochrane, Thomas Haas, East Bay Hotel.

Some of this material was previously published in WOMEN'S TIMES, Numbers 26, 27 and 34.

Front cover illustration is an oil painting by Ingeborg Holte, cover photography by Carol DeSain and cover design by Betsy Bowen.

Typesetting and production by Jane Lind. Printed by Arrowhead Printing, Superior, Wisconsin.

DEDICATION —

TO MOM AND DAD

Second Printing

CONTENTS

Ingeborg's Isle Royale

PART 1

AROUND THE ISLE

When the robins returned to the north woods and the chipmunk and black bear came out of hibernation and looked around at the magnificent new green of spring, Mama would announce it was that time of year again. So the big old trunk was hauled out of the attic, and the long tedious job of sorting and packing began. Going to live on Isle Royale every summer had many advantages, but this was not one of them. As our departure time approached, Mama's temper shortened, and my brother and I kept our distance from both Mama and the trunk.

Finally when it was stuffed to overflowing with all the family's needs for the summer, my brother and I sat on it to force the lid down. Mother would lock it and heave a big sigh. Her good nature returned, and she would tell all concerned in Swedish, "Yag spyta pa hela tingen, aldre bler da mera inti skal yag mova igen!" Translated: "I spit on the whole thing, never will there be more of this; never shall I move again!" She made this exclamation twice every year — moving to Isle Royale and coming back.

We were looking forward to being with Papa again. My father and all the other fishermen went to the Island just as soon as the ice broke up in Lake Superior. Most of them had families who joined them as soon as possible, usually when school let out. A few of the families did live on the Island year round, until Isle Royale became a national park in 1940, when this was no longer allowed.

Our belongings were loaded on to a dray, and we all headed for the passenger dock to await the arrival of the *SS America*. Our baggage made a large enough pile to sit on, and before long the *America* would come puffing very importantly into the harbor. We were always impressed by what we thought was an enormous passenger boat. Seen through the eyes of children, it looked huge. As we all scrambled aboard, Mama said, "Bless my soul, we made it again; once more we are on our way to Isle Royale."

The *America* freighted supplies, passengers and mail to various ports along the north shore, Canada and Isle Royale. It kept a regular schedule through the season, as long as Lake Superior stayed open, before the long winter freezeup.

The *America* was owned and operated by the Booth Fisheries. Unfortunately, for many years, this was the only company that bought fish from the fishermen all along the north shore and on Isle Royale. I expect it is unnecessary to add that there were no wealthy fishermen. Each fisherman's supplies and freight were delivered on account at the beginning of the season. As the fisherman sold fish to the company through the season, his credit was merely deducted from his account. Rarely did the fisherman or his family see cash. He was considered fortunate if his catches for the season covered the account of supplies laid in for the summer.

Although our best food was the delicious fresh trout and we kept a small garden, we did lay in quite a supply of food for the summer. Smoked ham kept pretty well, and cheesecloth soaked in vinegar was wrapped around the slab of bacon. Of course there was salt pork for the baked beans.

Fresh meat was brought to the Island and salted down in a barrel like corned beef. When a boiled dinner was planned, Dad would tie a rope around a chunk of beef and hang it by the dock, securely fastening it to a post. I used to watch the minnows nibbling around the edges. Eggs were packed in a barrel with rather coarse salt, and the butter was kept in large wooden tubs. I can still see the delicious slabs of butter being cut and brought in to the table, little beads of salt water glistening on the sides of it. Um — imagine that on fresh home baked rye bread!

Papa had built a small screened-in pantry in the fish house. The fish house was built over the water, so the air cooled by the cold Lake Superior water circulated through the pantry, and the food kept amazingly well in there.

Fish house at Wright Island

Most of our vegetables were brought to the Island at the beginning of the season, such as rutabagas, carrots, onions and potatoes, although we did have a small garden with patches of lettuce, carrots, beets and beans.

One year our garden produced a bumper crop. Unfortunately we had not fenced it, and one morning when we went out to admire it, it was gone. Every single plant. It remained a mystery what happened, although the beaver was looking biliously well-fed.

We did not get a lot of fresh fruit, only a barrel of apples that became smaller and more wrinkled as the season went on. And boxes of dried fruit such as raisins, prunes, peaches, apricots and pears. We kids were given these as special treats instead of candy. Our desserts were mainly bread, tapioca and rice puddings. Occasionally we'd have a custard that Mother called a brule. Cake was special and baked only for company.

I was very young, but I remember how the trout was kept fresh after it was caught and dressed (cleaned) until it could be put aboard the *America*. It was unheard of to have ice brought to the Island to keep the fish cold, so Papa did the next best thing. A sturdy rope was run through the jaws of the trout where the gills were removed and out through the mouth. Several trout were tied securely in this manner leaving a few fathoms of rope with a buoy tied to the end. These strings of fish were put into the icy cold water and left there until boat day, which was twice a week. The fish kept well and really looked fresh, especially when the blood along the backbone was cut and sort of spread around the innards. Occasionally the lake water became too warm for this method.

Then the only alternative was to salt the fish, so no one fished trout but concentrated on herring and menomenee because these fish were salted.

My father's own venture into fishing in this country was in the 1880's at Todd Harbor; he located on Green Isle. What I find so remarkable is that absolutely everything was handmade — even his first sailboat. The planks were cut and shaped from trees with an axe and a hand saw. He must have had a special feeling for that boat, as he talked about the planked lapstrake and the center board and how he sewed the sails using a large curved needle and an awl. He eventually bought a Mackinaw sailboat because he needed a larger one.

All the fishermen's equipment was handmade including floats (corks) and buoys. Leads were poured into molds. The net reels are always handmade as well as all the gadgets used in filling needles with twine and the needles themselves. At first the complete nets were handmade. Now you can buy the netting, but the cork and lead line have to be sewn on. This is called "seaming" nets.

In addition to building boats and making their equipment by hand, the fishermen also needed to build the log cabins, fish houses and the net and storage houses. The most important and hardest to build were the crib docks that could withstand the tide and storms. Everything was started by first cutting trees. In later years, logs from broken up "log booms" being towed by tugs on Lake Superior drifted into bays and harbors, and very few of these were salvaged by their owners. So when they dried they were used for building as well as for firewood. Mama did not think much of my father's style of handmade furnishings, however. Somehow everything looked suspiciously like fish boxes! I have managed to save one of his creations these many years, and it has a certain simplicity, like a Swedish modern!

Once in a while Papa would let me go along to the nets. A few trips were very scary to me as a small child, but yet I was always begging to go along. Papa never let a blow stop him. The sails came down only while he was lifting the nets. Then he would hoist them again, and soon we were going at a terrific speed with one side of the boat mostly at water level or in it and the other side up in the air — and that's where I would sit and yell. Papa said "ungen skriker som bara tusande" (the child hollers like a thousand).

After the *America* steamed out of Duluth, its homeport, the first stop was Two Harbors, which was my childhood hometown. At that time Two Harbors was a real booming city and had the largest ore docks in the country. The *America* made many stops along the shore before Grand Marais, unloading freight and taking on fish mostly from fishermen who came out to meet it. There were only two other stops at docks, at Schroeder and Tofte. Late in the afternoon we docked at Grand Marais, a beautiful little harbor with Maple Hill forming a backdrop for the village. When the *America* docked, some of the townsfolk would sit out on a point of rocks and make music on accordions, violins and guitars. I loved it, but as tourism moved in, the homely, unpretentious kinds of entertainment moved out. My husband was born in Grand Marais, and after our marriage, we lived there during

SS America

the winter months and spent the rest of the year on Isle
Royale.

Further along the shore, I remember the bustling little
fishing village of Chicago Bay, located near Hovland. Then
the last stop before we got to Thunder Bay in Canada (then
two cities named Port Arthur and Fort William) was Grand
Portage and the Susie Islands. This land of the voyageurs
around Grand Portage is still interesting to the traveler, with
the historic Stockade Fort and Great Hall preserved. The
America's stop at Grand Portage offered one of the most
impressive views of the north shore from the water: Mount
Rose, Maude and the beautiful Mount Josephine rise in
majesty — sentinels of the area's past glory. One can easily
imagine the voyageurs beaching their 40-foot Montreal canoes
at the mountains' feet and switching to the smaller canoes
which could be portaged and would be used on the inland lakes.

We children had real affection and respect for that grand old ship, the *America*. To us youngsters it was in the luxury liner class, with its real staterooms, a large lounge and a dining salon where real linen tablecloths and napkins were used. We could sit on either the bow deck or the stern deck, or we could even walk on the promenade deck and sneak a quick peek into the pilot house, where Captain Smith was usually at the wheel.

The lounge held the most fascination of all for us, because it had a piano which we could try to play, to the disgust of the passengers relaxing in the lounge. On one wall was a mural illustrating the poem, Hiawatha. There was also a music box toward the front of the lounge. We always hoped someone would play it, although this happened very rarely. We knew we would never get money to play it from Mama. "Such foolishness!"

Many years later when the *SS America* settled its tired old hull on the bottom of the lake after hitting a reef in Washington Harbor, I felt grief for the loss of a dear old friend.

A boat, a ship, is a personal thing. After you and your boat have survived the trials of a real storm together, there is a lasting bond between you. I know. I watched my husband say goodbye to his old boat, the "Slim." And he wept as he ran her up on the beach for the last time. "Slim" and he had been through unforgettable times together.

The *America* would cross over to Isle Royale from Canada. Our first sight of the Island was the Amygdaloid Channel, and we made our first stop on Amygdaloid Island. This northeastern shore of Isle Royale is dotted with islands, coves, lanes and bays in an intricate pattern. My father compared it with the grandeur that was Norway, with its famous fjords and the deep green forests of Sweden.

The Island is composed of just about every conceivable land formation, from steep perpendicular cliffs covered with gorgeous multicolored lichen plunging into the deep indigo blue of the water, to the many beaches where sometimes a precious stone is hiding. It is easy to imagine the glories of the past in the brooding stillness of its forests and shimmering beauty of its inland lakes. As a child I used to think of the Indians skimming along in their sleek canoes, and the miners and their families, and I wished very much that the children were still there.

Isle Royale — the incomparable Island. The creator molded it with a Master's hand. Isle Royale was made a national park to preserve its wilderness and natural beauty. The archipelago consists of over 200 islands surrounding Isle Royale and many more located in the inland lakes. There are so many fine harbors and bays to escape into away from a storm.

Soon we will stop at Belle Isle. There used to be five resorts on Isle Royale, and this was the first one we stopped at. Belle Isle is fairly large and was dotted here and there with cottages. The main lodge was quite pretentious, with an enormous stone fireplace made more interesting with a design of various semi-precious gems: thomsonites (prenites), greenstones and amethysts. It was rumored that this lodge even had a golf course and a tennis court. For some of the passengers, this was their destination, but for others this stop

was the way back to the mainland and home.

When the *America* backed away from the dock at Belle Isle and proudly headed for Blake Point, the easternmost point of Isle Royale, we passed one of the most memorable events of the trip for me. On the east point of Belle Isle stood a wigwam and beside it a very lovely Indian maiden. As we passed her, she raised her arm in a benevolent gesture of farewell, while shading her eyes with her left hand, she gazed into the distance. She had long black braids and her garb looked very authentic. She was tan with flashing dark eyes and very white teeth. Our boat went as close to shore as possible so we could admire this statuesque beauty. I was too young to inquire into the authenticity of this happening. But I had great fun believing it was a real Indian princess.

Excitement mounted as we continued on our way around Blake Point. We could see freighters going to or from Canada and Passage Island, the U.S. Coast Guard Station and Lighthouse. Passage Island's main value was as an aid to navigation through the treacherous waters around Isle Royale, but it also is home to many unusual plants including the American Yew.

Now we were on the south side of Isle Royale, heading for Tobin Harbor. There are many little islands scattered around the harbor, most of which belonged to "the summer people" who built snug little cabins on the islands. The shores of the harbor are heavily wooded, and as a child, I used to think the trees grew right out of the water.

On the largest island of this group there was a resort called "Tobins" operated by a family named Smith. There was one building here I remember well from my childhood: a small cabin close to the dock with "United States Post Office" printed in large letters across the front. The Smiths flew the American flag nearby, and this combination invariably gave me goose pimples when I saw it; it seemed so tremendously important.

The Smiths had some very lovely daughters who gathered on the dock, and as the *America* hove to, they burst into song, "T–O–B–I–N–S where the food is the rarist, and the girls are the fairest, T–O–B–I–N–S." My mother usually sniffed and snorted over this. She said, "Yag har set better smear och into slickat pa da." (I have seen better butter than that and never licked on it.)

There were fisherman families living at Tobin Harbor also who shipped their fish via the *America.* All supplies were unloaded there and picked up by the residents of the small islands.

Captain Smith eased his ship out of Tobin Harbor and around Scoville Point, and in a very short time we came to Snug Harbor and Rock Harbor Lodge. The post office was moved here after Tobins closed, and it is now the only resort remaining on Isle Royale. Leaving Snug Harbor, we stopped at yet another lodge on Davidson Island in the outer chain of islands that forms Rock Harbor Channel, Tourist Home, which was owned and operated by a Scandinavian family. We went on past Mott Island, which later became the national park headquarters.

There were several fishermen families living around Rock Harbor, and I loved to go there as a young girl, especially to

Tobins Harbor

visit my Uncle Mike and Aunt Nellie. Their daughter Laura was just a little older than I and there were also two sons, Melford and Arnold. When our family came to visit we had a great time with good music and lots of good food.

Arnold was a born musician, and he played all the nostalgic Scandinavian songs on his Hohner button accordion and sang them in a fine voice. He was just a very little boy with an amazingly big talent. And there was always lots and lots of delicious food — everything good to eat that you could think of. Uncle Mike was a hard working fisherman and a kind softspoken man. His wife Nellie kept her brood well-fed and clean which was no small achievement in those days without any conveniences at all. These two wonderful people are now a beautiful memory, and I feel a great sense of loss for those good old days.

During the late spring Ed always had to run his boat to Rock Harbor in the late afternoon, set his bait nets and sleep a few hours. At dawn he would lift his nets and start back for Wright Island which was about 18 miles away. That was a long run in those days, because a motor boat averaged about 6 to 8 miles an hour.

After he had a big breakfast, he would take off to his hook lines which were set many miles from the Outer Islands. This was no easy trip, especially during the early storms.

I was alone much of the time during this hook line season, but I had a wonderful friend and protector − a very intelligent dog who, because of his size we called "Big un." Everyone said the only thing he couldn't do was talk our language.

Shortly after our marriage we lived in the log cabin close to the water's edge where we could hear every boat come in. One morning while Ed was gone to his hook lines, there was a knock on our kitchen door. I was startled, because I had not heard a boat. In the early 30's there were very few cruisers or yachts around, and the sailboat had not made its comeback yet.

I was not afraid, however, because I trusted "Big un" to warn and protect me. I opened the door, and I could not believe my eyes. No one wore beards in those days, but here stood a man with the longest, wildest, fiery red beard and just as much hair to match. I forgot to close my mouth, and the stranger grinned and said, "Don't be frightened, lady, it's human."

This was too much for "Big un." My brave protector

had put his tail between his legs and fled to safety under the kitchen table.

The young man had come in a canoe, and like so many others, was interested in the ecology of the Island. He was interesting and very nice. Even "Big un" came to like him and sheepishly came out from under.

* * * * * * * * *

Joe was a very dear friend of ours who worked for the Park Service. He was captain of the "Tonawanda" tug, and his job was varied, at times becoming very strenuous during bad weather and fog. The old gentleman said he had ulcers, and his preferred diet was graham crackers and sardines!

One of his occasional duties was to cross Lake Superior to Houghton, Michigan on the south shore. Returning to Isle Royale on one of these trips, the fog closed in on the "Tonawanda," but it didn't really cause a problem for Joe until he was nearing Isle Royale. He had to navigate the entrance into Rock Harbor Channel where it becomes difficult to avoid the reefs entirely by reading the compass. Reefs pop up right in front of your boat. Sometimes Joe would, as we all did, turn off the engines and listen. If we could hear the cry of gulls, we would go slowly and look for reefs.

Joe had a ship to shore radio, and he used it. He called the park headquarters at Mott Island and asked about the fog conditions. The radio operator replied, "It's not so bad, Joe. I can see the moon." Joe's reply was a classic, "Hell, man, I'm not going to the moon!"

Just past Mott Island, at the western edge of Rock Harbor is Caribou Island where our family and many others congregated for 4th of July picnics for many years.

I must tell you about some of our fantastic 4th of July celebrations. Or perhaps I should say unbelievable. My older brother always managed to think of some way to get a keg of home brew set and working. Our closest neighbor's son was about the same age, and those two planned and connived weeks before that eventful day. On one Fourth, my father over-indulged, and he was completely flattened, verbally and physically. My mother wielded a broom with dexterity, at the same time lashing out with her tongue. Papa said, "Da vad den gongen, aldre min skhal blear da mer." "That was that time, but oh my soul, never again."

My mother heartily approved of prohibition and disapproved of home brew, so of course the utmost discretion had to be used by the brewers. Consequently, the keg of brew was well hidden in the woods. The only thing available in liquid refreshments at that time was a nonalcoholic drink called Near Beer. And it was heartily approved of, naturally, by Mama. So when the keg was put aboard our boat with the rest of the picnic goodies, on the morning of the Fourth, she did not suspect any skulduggery. My brother Steve and I knew better however, and we had a pretty good thing going for us the past weeks. We threatened to tell all unless we were paid off. My brother John thought this was a good joke, and he went along and gave us a penny or two occasionally and even a nickle a couple of times.

As sometimes happens when the left hand does not know

what the right hand is doing, the two brewers outfoxed one another. My brother managed via some .mysterious underground channel to buy a gallon of moonshine, and he poured this into the Near Beer. As the days passed and he got to thinking about it, he decided to negotiate for another jug, which he added to the brew. He thought that should just about do it. But he did not know that his partner, the neighbor's son, had secretly added the same amount of dynamite to the keg.

The entourage consisting of all the boats within the range of about ten miles headed for the same destination: the picnic on Caribou Island where a dance platform had been erected. The weather was perfect. The Chippewa Indians called the 4th "the white man's big rainy Sunday," but that day they were wrong. In fact it was so nice and warm, everyone became quite thirsty, and as the day progressed everyone agreed that it was very fortunate that they had that keg of Near Beer along!

The pavilion was really jumping as the dancers became more and more boisterous. Some of the more ambitious ones tried new dance steps to the amusement of the onlookers. The woods and rocky shores rang with the echoes of polkas, waltzes, Hambos and the schottische. Many of the songs were sung in Swedish and Norwegian. By that time most everyone was aware that this was no ordinary Near Beer. It was too late for the teetotalers to withdraw with any dignity, in fact for some of them it was practically impossible.

We did not get home until the following day. Everyone said it was too rough out there. There were several rocky members in the crew, so there was a unanimous decision to wait for the disturbance to subside. Besides my big brother and his buddy were eager to put off the inquisition as long as possible.

There were times when we could not join the revelers in celebrating the 4th of July. As our parents became older they became less interested in such nonsense. I remember one instance my husband and I have chortled over many times. One of the fishermen who lived in the Big Bay area stopped by our place on his way home from the celebration. He was still in a gay mood, as he put it, "Ya du, men ve have got da fort of yuly yet." Sooo, on with the dance! In a very courtly fashion he asked if I would honor him with a dance, and of course I accepted. With a look of glee, my husband put a long playing record on the old phonograph. We danced on and on. My partner was a good dancer, but the hours of revelry had taken their toll. His dancing was becoming a punishment for his aching legs, and he was huffing and puffing and flapping his arms like an injured loon. He was made of sterner stuff however, and besides a gentleman did not return his partner to her seat until the music stopped. Finally in desperation he turned to Ed and said, "Chare Gud, Stup de damn ting." The glow was gone from our friend, and he decided to return to his home. He walked disconsolately to his boat, grumblingly addressing the world in general, "A man iss no dem gud ven he is up to fifty." We knew the old gentleman was getting his social security checks.

Leaving Caribou Island, the scene of our festivities, we glide past the Rock Harbor Lighthouse, an old weathered structure that had been used during the mining days. This relic is still in use today, as a museum by the National Park Service.

Soon we were steaming out of there, around Saginaw Point, and before long we were at Chippewa Harbor. To me this is without a doubt the most beautiful place on Isle Royale: with its cliffs rising toward the sky and evergreens growing on the ridges. There is a low sandy field where many Indian artifacts were found and where once stood the log cabin that we lived in for several years before we moved to Wright Island, our permanent residence. One can almost see the canoes of the Chippewa Indians skimming through the water, paddles flashing in the sunlight and rippling through reflections made by the overhanging cliffs.

Our place at Chippewa Harbor – circa 1891

I am not at all sure that our log cabin at Chippewa Harbor was built by my father. More than likely it was already there and Papa just moved in. That was the custom of the fishermen. If a place were abandoned, they had no compunction about moving in or taking what they needed to build their own homes. Materials were hard to come by on the Island and expensive to freight over from the mainland. So the houses abandoned by the mining company were reused by the fishermen. When one fisherman left the Island, his cabin was quickly torn down and moved by another fisherman or just moved into.

My father lived at three other places before coming to Chippewa Harbor. First at Little Boat Harbor, then Green Isle in Todd Harbor and then at Caribou Island.

Long before I was born Mama went back to Sweden because her mother was very ill. Besides being very lonesome in this strange land, she had an urgent desire to see her mother once more before "leaving this vale of tears," as she put it. My older sister Alice was still at the "carrying age," and Mama was pregnant, but undaunted. My brother John was born in Sweden, and it was five long years before Papa made enough money to get them back again.

On their trip back the ship's doctor discovered a few remaining scars from chicken pox on Alice's legs. So mother and children were put off the ship in Ireland, and there they remained until the pox scars were completely gone.

Naturally there was a language barrier, but Mama learned to like the Irish people sincerely. Being the religious person she was, she was most impressed by their love for their church.

The Irish she knew were devout Catholics, and absolutely nothing interfered with their time of worship. Mama often recalled the time when the lady of the house where she and the children were boarding was scrubbing the floor when the church bell began ringing. This was obviously a call to worship, and this good woman, not wanting to be late, wiped her hands on her apron and quickly swished out the door, throwing the apron as she went. In her haste, she forgot that she had pinned up her skirt and the several petticoats, and there, exposed for the world to see, on a pair of full bloomers covering her posterior, was an advertisement for an excellent brand of flour.

Mother could understand using flour sacks to make bloomers; she made ours out of bleached sacks. My favorite was a brand that featured a cute little sunbonnet girl. There was an iron-clad rule regarding these particular undies, however, we were not supposed to brag about wearing them! Obviously they were not creations to be

Mama and me at Chippewa Harbor

proud of. They were always dried indoors, out of sight.

When Mother finally was able to leave Ireland and come back, she found her children wanted to remain in the old country. In the first place, they were sure they could not find America, and secondly, they had no idea who or what their father was like: John had never seen him and Alice had forgotten him. Mama told them that when they got to where Papa was they would be in America. On their arrival at Chippewa Harbor they were told by their mother that this man was their father. They looked around them in obvious surprise and said in Swedish, "So, nu ar vi i America." So, now we are in America." It was immediately obvious that these two immigrants from Sweden had no intention of minding their father. It was all a big joke to them, which caused much amusement as well as exasperation.

As we headed west from Chippewa, we came into Siski-wit Bay. We could see Menagerie Island with its old light-house. This is the easternmost island in the chain that forms the outer bank of Siskiwit Bay, and it is composed almost entirely of perpendicular rock cliffs harboring many vari-colored lichens. The old lighthouse is built from native stone which had become covered with lichens, mostly orange in color.

I do not remember the elder Malones at all. Mr. Malone was lighthouse keeper for many years, and I remember my father talking about him when I was young. My memories of the Malones are of his son Al, and later on, Al's wife Gertie.

Visiting with Al Malone at Menagerie Island was probably comparable to going to Disneyland for the children nowadays. There was a well-tended lawn around the lovely old lighthouse and many wild rose bushes. A cement walk extended from the house to the west end of the island, where there was a large boat house and dock. Part of the wonder of this place to us kids was the cement walk (instead of a trail) and the huge house made of stone. All this in an almost complete wilderness!

To add to this Al Malone treated me like a princess. He took my hand and tucked it into the crook of his arm as we strolled up the walk and into the immense three story house. He would lead me right up to the organ and gallantly bowing he would seat me on the stool and request a song. I would warble away like a bird, I thought, and energetically plunk on the organ. I imagined I was doing a bang up job. When I grew older I realized this was not the accepted form of music, and my friend Al was no less a saint to endure this with a smile of approval.

I also loved to watch the barn swallows that nested in the boat house; there seemed to be hundreds of them. The sound of their wings surrounded me as I stood quietly watching them, making a quick swishing prup prup sound, similar to bat wings. Another point of interest was an elegant platform with a fancy railing around it, extending out from a cliff. A contraption was used to lower a rope with a pail attached. When this pail hit the water, it would naturally fill up and the "water boy" would haul it up by rewinding the rope. Very simple and very efficient.

After the light was maintained by batteries, the Malones left the lighthouse on Menagerie Island and moved to an island close to the mainland, which of course was named after them, as was the bay it was situated in. They tried to make a living by fishing, and they built a couple of log cabins with the idea of having a resort. After a few years without much success, the Malones left Isle Royale. So, to my regret, the Malones became just one more fond memory.

There were several fishermen and their families living on Hat Island in Malone Bay at that time. One family brought their own cow along. This docile creature would allow herself to be rowed in a skiff from one island to another to supplement her diet. We were always amused by her. After a while she ignored the skiff and began swimming to her destination. Wonder if she met any moose enroute!

Wright Island, which is only a short distance from Malone Island, is our next stop. After living in four different locations on Isle Royale, my father finally decided this was it. I remember the day we moved. It seems like an impossible feat to me now, but at that time this all seemed so routine. On that eventful day when we were moving ten miles away, there was a light breeze blowing. We did not get far, only about a mile, when the wind died down. All our worldly goods were in that boat in addition to the whole family, which weighed it down considerably. Papa rowed and rowed, on and on, hour after hour, and when the dear man stopped I would ask him, "Var for roer du inte Papa?" "Why do you not row, Papa?"

All day he rowed until finally we reached our destination in the late afternoon. I looked upon this island with great expectations, because Papa had promised us there would be no blackflies and no snakes. This was a tall order, but being a kind man, and knowing his children were unhappy about leaving Chippewa, he knew this would help. I knew we would miss the old familiar haunts, the hill where grew the delicious sweet strawberries and the sand beach where we could go swimming, nude, without ever being disturbed by people. But I was fed up with picking water snakes out of my pockets, put there by my little brother, and of course the sneaky blackflies bit the daylights out of us.

Our new home was on the scenic Wright Island, which is made up of three bays or harbors, the smallest of which we naturally called, "Little Harbor." There was a calm reflected beauty there from the changing sky and color of the dark evergreens: a stillness, a waiting, a mystic quality that fills your being with contentment, a closeness to God.

Nothing was more excitingly beautiful than watching Papa's return from the nets. His two-masted Mackinaw sailboat would come into sight around a rocky point. Sometimes with sails unfurled and billowing in the wind. I wanted to shout, "Home is the victor!" Over the season, unfortunately, there were many days when those sails hung limp and useless. There were no auxiliary motors in those days, so when the winds were becalmed, the fishermen rowed many miles to and from their nets.

There were other families living in this Siskiwit Bay area. We did not see them very often because we always had to go by boat, and in those days our boats did not exceed any speed limits. The words, "going visiting" caused

Fishing on the lake in 1890

much excitement among the Island families. To us youngsters it meant new worlds to explore. It meant at least one day of preparations. This always included a scrubbing from head to foot in a washtub that was much too small. One felt like a pretzel looked, and heaping insult on injury a bucket of clear water, sometimes cold, was dumped over us to rinse the soap off. Of course we all donned clean clothes from the skin out. I could never understand why all the fuss. How could anyone appreciate all this cleanliness? Especially when it was all covered up. Phooey.

But my mother felt very strongly about this because she said there was always a possibility of someone being injured, and one had just better be prepared to be exposed, including our underclothes, etc. One could even fall overboard, almost drown, and of course be rescued, and think of the terrible disgrace of not being dressed for such an emergency. She did look a little sheepish after that last threat, and even she had to admit she was carrying things a little too far.

Then there was all that food to prepare to take along. This was pretty silly too. Unless the lady of the house that you intended to visit was prostrate and could not lift a finger, you were not permitted to contribute one crumb of your food. I do not know why this custom was established, but it was not at all practical in the days when boats did not have cabins or spray hoods. If the lake were rough or if it rained, the food would probably be inedible. Oddly though, much todo and clucking was done over the food brought by the visitors, even though it was rarely taken out of the boat. I was greatly puzzled by this behavior and asked my mother about it. She seemed very surprised at my ignorance and stated flatly that any nincompoop should understand that. So I never did find the answer.

Excitement mounted and finally the moment arrived when Papa yelled "All aboard!" We kids scrambled into the boat and turned our attention to watching Mama sally forth from our log cabin. To her two small children she looked terrific. Like a prima donna maybe. Papa said she resembled a ship under full sail. He would take her hand as she stepped gingerly into the boat and seated herself in the bow on a recently-scrubbed seat. She saw no reason why she should not wear her very best clothes. A very elegant hat with a high crown covered with flowers and a mauve veil. Luckily the veil kept most of the flowers from blowing off and into the lake. Her coat was very impressive, with a tight-fitting waist and leg-of-mutton sleeves. She also wore kid gloves. The works . . . even to her patent leather slippers. The fact that the boat smelled of fish and there were a few fish scales here and there, seemed most unimportant to Mama.

We loved the ride across the Big Bay, and finally we rounded the point and went into a calm little cove. Our destination. We would have a few hours to visit with another fishing family. There were children our age to play with and new territory to explore. The afternoon went all too quickly, and it was time for us to cross the Big Bay again on our trip home. We were entertained royally with an excellent dinner and a promise to return again, soon. We knew, however, that we would be real lucky if we could do this again, just once more that summer. There was so little time for frivolity. Back in our own beds and safely tucked away, we relived the day, our imaginations going beyond that calm little cove.

Traveling by boat has changed completely in the recent years. Speed has become very important, allowing at least one benefit: the ability to outrun an approaching storm. In comparison our boats were very slow, but we liked that for several reasons. We could enjoy the shoreline and the other sights at our leisure. Our boats would ease themselves over the waves without any fuss, and we could travel in stormy weather more easily than the faster boats.

The fishermen named many of the places around Isle Royale, usually with descriptive, self-explanatory names. A good example is the island which is located south of Wright

Island which is not protected from the winds and so very cold, as a family found out when they tried to live there. This island was named Shiverette — what else?

Uncle Mike and my father whose name is Sam began their fishing career together, and Mike had a special talent for naming places. There are two very shallow reefs located in an unexpected place, where fishing is very risky and often disastrous. But, as is often the case, the fishing was good, so Sam and Mike went right on trying to fish those reefs. Mike derived a little satisfaction by naming them "Doden och Domen," Death and Doom.

A reef running out from Crow Point is called Gilbertson's Farm: a strange name for a reef, but a man named Gilbertson always set his nets there, and it became a very productive "farm."

Another name which needs no explanation is Starvation Point, which is located near Rock Harbor. You are so right — no fish there.

Washington Harbor has a Bubbly Point, and some day I hope to find out why. There is a Blind Creek in Siskiwit Bay, so named because you cannot see it; the mouth is so well camouflaged. Yet another point is called Checker Point, after the two fishermen who vied with each other for the best sets. This resembles the game of Checkers as one tries to outwit the other with certain strategic maneuvers.

My brother Steve and I considered ourselves to be two very fortunate youngsters. Before the cares of growing up caught up to us, our summer days were filled with adventure. We usually played at fishing in the harbor with Papa's worn out nets.

We formed a fish company, and since I was two years younger and a girl, of course I was the junior member. I was permitted to function at certain menial tasks, such as rowing the big heavy skiff with oars that were so large I could barely maneuver them. I adored my brother and he tolerated me. He took the title of Captain, and he played his role very realistically.

Because our fishing operation had to be conducted under the watchful eyes and ears of our mother, our fish company was operating mostly in the red. And it was very demeaning to be permitted to go no further than about twenty feet away from the dock to set our nets. We rarely caught a fish. (Only trout were considered to be fish, and our catches consisted mostly of suckers and burbots and an occasional menomenee.)

The entire operation came to an abrupt halt one day when my brother, after being admonished several times by Mama for swearing at me like a real captain we knew, let fly with a mess of cuss words that would put any captain to shame. We were grounded for about two weeks. And I suppose it was just a coincidence that the raspberries were ripe, and we were told that if we behaved ourselves we would be allowed to pick them.

West of Wright Island and further up the bay, we come to Hay Bay where there were several families living in a well-protected little harbor. At the end of the harbor is the mouth of a little stream where some very nice brook trout and rainbows were caught. These men supported their families by fishing and growing some vegetables. They remained on the Island summer and winter, until it became necessary to move the children to the mainland to go to school.

During the winters they would see quite a few wild animals. The regal moose would walk past their cabin, following the trail to the lake, and wolves were often nearby. One time our neighbor waded through the snow to the outhouse, and after scooping all the snow off the seat, he settled down to the job at hand. All at once the air was filled with the sound of wolves howling. This is an awe-inspiring sound, and it so delighted our friend that he thought he would respond with a few well rendered howls of his own. To his surprise, his imitations were so good the wolves came down the hill behind the outhouse, looking for the origin of this new sound in wolf music. Our friend fled post haste toward his cabin, his suspenders and britches flapping in the breeze.

Another winter, another time, but the same place, our neighbor was grumbling because the night was very dark and cold and it was such a nuisance to go out in the cold to the biffy, and on top of everything else he had forgotten the flashlight. He was about to ease himself into a sitting position, when he remembered to brush off any snow which might be there. To his alarm, his hand touched something warm and furry! He did not linger. Clutching his trousers, he made it to the house in two jumps, flung open the door and yelled, "Is the cat out?" It was.

Other neighbors lived nearby, a pair of old Norwegian fishermen who shared a log cabin and cooked their meals together. There is nothing left there now but memories, and here and there a Sweet William, growing out of the past.

We had a good chuckle thinking back to those days, when these two fishermen generally got along fine. But one morning, one of the gentlemen was shocked to discover that his buddy, who had been cooking the daily eggs, was not washing them. Cripes, imagine boiling unwashed eggs! He was certainly not about to endanger his health eating dirty eggs. The culprit gazed at him in stunned silence and then emitted the bellow of an outraged wounded bull. "Herrie Gud," he said, "Ar du crazy?" Never in all his born days had he been so insulted or heard of such crap. With the little dignity left him, he walked out the door of the cabin, and that day he began to build his own log home. Of course each one told the story differently, but it did boil down to one thing: the partners were no longer cooking eggs together.

When Isle Royale became a national park, the residents were given a choice: sell their property and move off the Island or take a life lease.

Most of the fishermen took the lease because they not only had their investments in commercial fishing, but also had made their homes on the Island.

Most of the summer home people accepted life leases also. Oddly enough the ones who were active in establishing Isle Royale as a national park moved off the Island, complaining that they did not like the restrictions placed on them.

One of those restrictions was the outlawing of pets. An elderly couple who lived about six miles from us had kept a dog and a cat for many years. They loved these animals, and it was extremely difficult for them to realize they were not allowed to keep them.

So, for as long as they could, these old people tried to hide their pets whenever they heard or saw a boat coming into the bay.

There had been a terrible forest fire in 1936, and most of the money which had been allotted to establish Isle Royale as a park had been spent fighting that fire. So by now the park personnel consisted of only a skeleton crew, and most of the members were very informal. Park service boats were scarce and unmarked, so when the new superintendent (whom the woman had never met) stopped at their dock, both residents were in the fish house along with the cat.

The missus emerged from the house with cat following her, and since the gentleman looked very ordinary to her, she informed her pet, "It's okey dokey, Kitty. Dis ain't nobody; it's yust another yentleman." This woman's English was never very choosey. She said, "Tank da Gud you air not dat new park superintendent. I hierd his is a sin of a bits and I vudn't vant dat bistard to know someting about my kitty here."

The superintendent chose to remain anonymous, and after exchanging greetings, he left the old couple and their cat.

Having understanding and a good sense of humor were certainly a requirement for that job during those early years when the park was becoming established.

When leaving Siskiwit Bay, boats must go out through a channel which is very well marked because there are ledges of rock jutting out and forming a reef on either side of it. Navigation of the channel becomes very difficult in rough weather, because a strong current works against the sea, building monumental waves during a storm. In our small 18-foot boat, I felt very inconsequential, like a small wooden cork tossed into eternity. There is no doubt in my mind then who is in the driver's seat, in charge of my destiny. The unleashed forces of nature can remove a person's conceit very rapidly.

The *America* was much too large a boat to maneuver in and out of most of these small bays and coves, and the water near the fishermen's docks was far too shallow to allow the *America* to come near. So most of the fishermen piled their boxes of fish into their boats and went out to meet the big ship, sometimes in fog and storm. I was permitted to tag along occasionally, and I always enjoyed seeing the gaily dressed passengers at the bow of the ship.

Heading west around Houghton Point brings us into Fisherman's Home Cove. This is a little harbor, well protected, but with a very narrow entrance making it quite a challenge to some navigators. It requires a steady hand at the wheel and the knowledge of where not to go!

The channels and reefs are well-marked with buoys, yet there are times during a storm or a heavy fog when a boat could run aground. One instance I remember well because it involved about 20 sea scouts. Their boat was a rebuilt cabin cruiser of ancient vintage which had been donated to them. It was quite seaworthy, however. The skipper was a dedicated nice young man who was interested in teaching the boys how to handle a boat as well as the finer points of navigation. They came across Lake Superior from the south

Ed Holte

shore, and Isle Royale was their destination. Everything went fine until they neared the south shore of Isle Royale, and then their engine stopped and they could not get it started again. The boat began to drift into huge breakers, which can be extremely dangerous. One breaker lifted the boat over one shallow reef and set it down with a whomp on another. It was aground, yet in a precarious position. You can never imagine the feeling of desperation unless you have been there, which accounts for the decision made to get help.

A good rule for boating, especially when many people are involved is to have a life boat either towed or carried aboard. This cruiser had one. Two very capable youngsters managed to cross the Big Bay in it, operating the outboard motor successfully. I remember the southwester was about a 30-mile wind, and we were amazed to see two very young boys come into our dock asking for help.

Ed left at once in our 22-foot work boat, taking a heavy towing rope along. It is seven miles across the Siskiwit Bay and it seemed forever before I saw our boat come around the point towing the distressed cabin boat. It was almost dark when Ed maneuvered the helpless cruiser into Wright's, and they decided they had had enough adventure for one day. They spent the night with us, sleeping in the lower cabin, wherever they found room for their sleeping bags.

Ed was very handy with engines, and before too long he had repaired the engine on the cabin cruiser. The following morning the sea scouts took off to complete their voyage. About a month later Ed received an enormous box of chocolates and a magnificent thank you card signed by all the boys. He loved it, but he said the real heroes that day were the two lads who braved the storm and crossed the Big Bay in a very small boat.

This is not an unusual rescue story. In fact it was fairly common for the commercial fishermen to help fellow boaters. Their fishing grounds almost overlapped, so sometime during their working hours while lifting and setting nets, a boat in distress was bound to be seen and helped by one or more of them.

Sooner or later everyone got to know the Rudes at Fisherman's Home Cove. Sam and Elaine were an example of the real hospitality that was extended to those who are looking for information, seeking shelter from a storm, or to those who are just good old friends.

Before the Rudes came to live at Fisherman's Home, and during my youth when our comings and goings were via the *America,* another fisherman and his family spent many seasons there. He was a quiet reserved person, soft spoken, and as Mama said, "He had religion." When things went wrong for this man, he did not cuss, he prayed. And there was a rumor about him, that this fisherman was rich. Actually

Dad with trout

I believe "comfortably situated" would be more like it, but either way, having enough money was unheard of among the fishermen.

My mother tried with all her might to make Father into a duplicate of our neighbor, a religious man, because how could you fail with that kind of a setup?

My father was kind, sweet and very soft-hearted. He did not harm anyone or anything. He used to say he could not kill a fly, which was ironic to me, because every day for at least the half of every year, he killed fish. This did not bother him in the least. I guess he did not think of them as living animals. To him they were cold-blooded vertebrates, in a class by themselves, and put there specifically for him to catch.

He also claimed to be an agnostic. When he lost his nets during a bad storm, or the other fellows were getting good catches of fish and he was not, Mother would give him some knowing glances and several hurrumphs. Obviously things did not go well with a non-believer!

Most of the fishermen were Norwegians, and their forebears were fishermen in the old country. My husband's father was a fisherman in Norway, as was his father before him. The same proud traditions were carried on my side also — only my family is Swedish. The call of the sea is always there. The feeling of exultation courses through one's veins as the bow of the boat neatly divides the water in two or cuts through a wave, or sometimes glides up one side of a gigantic mound and down the other. We can watch the beginning of the dawn, the beginning of life as we glide into the front pew. I think there is some of the spirit of the Vikings in these Nordic fishermen. Perhaps it is only a memory, but the melody lingers on.

My father used to say, "All you get out of this damn job is an empty belly and a wet ass," but absolutely nothing this side of heaven could keep him away from it.

Leaving Fisherman's Home we waited at Long Point for the fishermen to come out to the *America*. As a child I remember the very elegant 'uptown' house that was built there. It had a glassed-in front porch and real hardwood flooring. Part of the building was of native stone and very impressive. Unhappily it was abandoned when one of the owners died, so of course another fishery was through. Many of these fishing places that have been evacuated are eventually destroyed by the Park Service because they have become hazards to safety.

Remembering these old log cabins brings a feeling of sadness and nostalgic memories of days gone by. The weeks, the months, the years, the sweat and yes, the tears that went into making them homes. Where children laughed, played and fought, and grew up among the wonders of nature, learning that all this splendor is as one with its Creator.

We finally come to the last stop, Washington Harbor, which is located on the western end of Isle Royale. This was a bustling place with several fisheries and two resorts. Windigo, which is the name of the present resort, was once a private club.

Singer's Resort, which used to be located on Washington Island, has been closed for many years. This resort was famous for its furnishings of gorgeous antiques brought there from all over the world. Some of these priceless pieces were actually given away to the neighboring residents; no one seemed to realize the monetary value of them in those days.

The Sivertson family lived on the west end of Washington Island, and I have many happy memories of enjoying visits with them there. It was a day to remember when we had the good fortune of being invited to have some of that fine lady's very special fishcakes. Nothing has ever tasted as good before or since.

Having gone to live on Isle Royale every year since I was born until now at 82, I know with a deep feeling of gratitude that it has been my privilege to live among all this beauty these many years.

Our cabins at Wright Island

PART 2

AMONG THE WILDLIFE

Plant and animal ecology were not taught in our schools when I was a child, but I was more fortunate than most, because I grew up among many interesting and beautiful wild animals. Many of those creatures either moved off the Island because of the lack of food, or were killed by predators.

I remember the stately caribou and the lynx. Also there were martin and fisher. None of these remain. There are the mink, moose, otter and fox. Of the smaller animals, the snowshoe hare and the red squirrels are fairly abundant. The brush wolves seemed to disappear after the timber wolves came. There are many opinions regarding the dates when these various animals came to Isle Royale. Because there are no hibernating animals, the theory goes that most of them crossed over on the ice. It is also possible for the moose to swim a long distance. The deer were imported by the Washington Harbor Club, which was located at Windigo many years ago. Of course the deer are no longer there either.

The moose remain at a good level, although there is some doubt as to the possibility of there being enough browse for them if their numbers should increase. The balance is pretty well maintained by just the right number of timber wolves who seem to have the insight or instinct to keep their pack at the right level also. The number of wolves apparently is regulated by the number of moose.

Of all the animals one can encounter on Isle Royale, the moose seem to be the most interesting and the most memorable. For many visitors, just to spot a moose or two at a distance can be the highlight of their trip. Living in the wild as we did for so many years, we had several encounters with moose — some just a little more intimate than we might like.

* * * * * * * * *

The sun glistened on the dark wet fur of a cow moose and her young calf. They stood together silhouetted against the aquamarine of lake and sky, making a small ripple in the shallow pool which reflected the beauty of these large animals. Moose are surprisingly graceful; I have watched them daintily pick their way through a meadow of buttercups without destroying a single small flower.

There are weeds growing in the shallow water in Hopkins Bay which is directly across from our cabin. Watching these huge animals disappear into the lake and minutes later emerge chewing on a mouthful of plants is an amazing sight. My father used to call this green delicacy "Neptune's sheg" (beard) and "squirrel tails." He also called them less lyrical names when they made a tangled mess of his nets during a northeast blow.

The bull moose who now stood by in polite and dignified deference was not eating. This was definitely a gourmet meal he was passing up — why? For the same reason the nearby beaver lodge was getting a repair job done on the roof by

Moose painting by Ingeborg Holte

one member of the family, while another member sat on a small beach beside the lodge complacently scratching her belly. Even though it is impossible to tell the sex of a beaver from outward appearance, there was no doubt in my mind which was which that day: the roof patcher was definitely a gentleman and the lady fair sitting on the beach was his mate. Or is it possible that this was only a figment of my imagination?

I noted with approval that other females were given preference on this day too. For instance — me. My husband casually mentioned that it was 'mother's day' and a beautiful morning — two very good reasons for a picnic on Little Greenstone Beach. Ah, the riddle was solved. Following the example of my furry friends, I decided to take advantage of this day also.

After donning the usual cold weather gear, we set out on a day of anticipation. Would this be the day we would find that perfect gem? We did not have to travel far. Our cabin on Wright Island is only about six miles from Little Greenstone Beach. Our boat meandered through the channels, past picturesque little islands, through narrows, into a perfect harbor, then out into the open waters. At our leisurely pace we could watch the progress of a brood of mergansers, spot a loon nest on an island ledge, watch a busy beaver adding a fresh stick to its home, or view the ever glorious swoop of a herring gull.

We eased our 18-foot motorboat, the "Tern," through shallow water and into a snug cove. We never tired of this familiar and beautiful place, of looking around at the grandeur of the perpendicular rock cliffs covered with moss and lichen, and the grey-green pebbles of the beach edged with the clear water of the lake.

After Ed secured the boat, he walked to the far end of the beach. I found a nice spot closer to the boat. We each had our favorite locations in which to look for the elusive greenstone.

I was enjoying myself at the water's edge. It was the kind of day that gives new meaning to life and to every growing thing. The warm sun and the lazy lapping sounds of the waves along the beach were making me drowsy, and I was just about to exchange rock collecting for a nap when suddenly a strange sound came from behind me. It was a soft sound, yet peculiarly urgent. I turned around and saw a cow moose standing at the edge of the woods. She was looking at me intently, and her large long ears were bent forward. Moose have very poor eyesight, but their senses of smell and hearing are exceptionally keen. Unfortunately I did not know that she was looking for her calf, which was nowhere in sight.

We know a cow moose is a good mother, and we know to keep a sizable distance between ourselves and her recently born calves. A calf remains with its mother for about one year, during which the mother teaches it how to survive. This well-protected offspring becomes a yearling under the mother's watchful eye. But just before another calf is born, the mother drives the yearling away from her with surprising fury and deadly purpose. During that first year, it is downright dangerous to get between a cow and her calf. Usually a placid cud chewer, she becomes very protective and has been known to cause a few curious people to scramble up a nearby tree — or even a sapling.

I recall the adventure of three young friends who leapt upon a poor little unsuspecting aspen which was the only available perpendicular object in the vicinity. The boys were fishing along the Siskiwit River when they thought they heard an "advancing bull moose." One of the boys climbed up to the top of the little tree, which immediately bent over almost touching the ground. The lad straddling the middle was in the best spot, but the poor kid trying to get off the ground kept yelling, "Help!" and in desperation, he clutched the firmest looking object within reach — his friend's britches — and yanked. He never did get off the ground, but he did get his buddy's pants. To their surprise and chagrin they discovered the "moose" was only a skiff being rowed around a point. Any self-respecting moose would have died laughing at this ridiculous sight.

For me, seeing a moose was rather common and nothing to be afraid of, so I turned to the job at hand. About a minute later I heard the sound of rocks rolling down the beach and instinctively I had a feeling of panic. I swiftly turned around and froze — she was coming toward me. As she came closer her hair rose on the nape of her neck and along her back. Her eyes rolled backward showing only the whites, and she drew her lips away from large white teeth. To her I was an enemy, and her feeling of helpless frustration turned to anger.

As she came closer she reared back on her hind legs, pawing the air and then coming down with a thump. I had no idea why she directed all this fury at me, but I decided to get moving and fast. Then as I stumbled to my feet I realized that I was paralyzed with fear, and my legs would not hold me up. Now I knew real fear. I was reduced to a blubbering mess. I wept, crawled and yelled. Or at least I thought I did, but it came out a whimper. Ed told me later that he did not hear me. Someone, something made him look in my direction just in time, and he came to my rescue.

I could feel her anger lashing out at me. In that agonizing moment I knew this wild unhappy creature could kill me if she wanted to with one blow of her hooves. It is silly, but I felt as though a lifelong friend had turned against me. I had grown up with the big, homely, yet magnificent creatures. They fed on the soft maples that grow around our cabin and the weeds that thrive in the shallow water of the little harbor nearby. Perhaps that is why I like to believe

58

she let me live. Most likely though the real reason is that a moose is not a killer by nature. They prefer to live and let live, mostly browsing and raising their young.

We learned a great deal about the behavior of the moose that day. When Ed stood up and started toward her, she was startled. She turned around and made a complete circle before returning to her pursuit of me. It seemed that she was only capable of concentrating on one thing or person at a time. We were grateful — it gave me a chance to escape. Ed tugged, pushed and finally hauled me up the side of the cliff at the west end of the beach. I crawled into a small cave left by long ago miners. I felt safe for the present, but we knew there was a less steep approach to the cliff, and the moose could easily come up that way. During the four hours that we were there she did not attempt to do so.

As the afternoon sun moved toward the west, the mosquitoes were coming out. We watched the moose, pacing back and forth below us. Occasionally she would look up at Ed, who was standing most of the time, as if to remind us that she had not forgotten we were there. She showed her anger by pawing the beach with her front hooves. At times she was calm, and standing at the water's edge she stretched her head forward looking out over the lake and made soft little sounds, almost like calling and calling.

We felt her grief, and in spite of our dilemma we could only feel pity for her. The long winter had taken its toll. Her hip bones stood out sharply, and large patches of fur were gone from her sides.

At the time we could not understand her behavior.

Obviously we were not between her and her calf. She was not very large; we thought she could be a yearling who had been driven away by her mother. These unhappy creatures are frightened and unpredictable until they gain some self-confidence. At times we thought she had forgotten about us as she stood at the edge of the woods and her sides heaved in and out and she calmly chewed her cud. Wish we had a built-in lunch counter like that, instead of the conventional kind, now unattainable in our boat.

We had to begin thinking seriously about the new menace, the mosquitoes. The monsters were trying to devour us. Ed wanted to circumvent the area and hopefully get the boat along the cliff to a lower area where I could get into it. This plan was good — except that I was scared witless and would not budge from my safe little cave, and worse yet, I would not stay there alone.

While sitting there and wistfully looking out at the clear water, I made a discovery. That large boulder which had only the top of it sticking out of the water had legs, long thin little legs. So — we were between this mother and her calf after all. We knew then that the calf could have been born on the beach that day, and the poor little fellow had staggered around on wobbly legs and into the icy water and drowned. Anyone entering the scene that day would have been an enemy. The mother's voice, calling to her dead calf was coaxingly tender. I felt tears sting my eyes because being a supposedly superior being, I knew her calf was dead. She still had hope.

After sitting cramped in the little cave for four hours,

we decided to move to a larger cave further down the cliff and build a fire. We hoped the smoke would discourage the mosquitoes. I eased out of the little cave and stood up. My movement startled the moose, and she kicked up her hind legs and took off like a shot into the woods. This reinforced our belief that she concentrated on only one thing at a time. She had been watching Ed because he was standing up and moving. We realized that although she did not go as far as we had hoped she would (she was still clearly visible) it was now or never.

We scrambled down the side of the cliff. Our destination, the "Tern," looked many miles away to me. Ed ran at an angle, heading for the tree where our boat was tied. I headed for the boat — taking the shortest route. This time I had no trouble getting into the boat. I hit the deck flat on my stomach and climbed quickly into the stern. Ed was right behind me, giving the boat a mighty heave as he leapt into it. What a relief as we slowly drifted away from shore. Ed started the motor, and as we were backing away, I noticed I was clutching a rock in one hand and a stick in the other! We had a shaky laugh over that. My puny defense against that huge wild creature.

We had no sooner left the beach when the cow returned. We made another discovery about the habits of the moose. She tracked us like almost any other animal will do, by sniffing where we had walked along the beach to the boat. Somehow we did not expect an animal that large would be that average. We left her then as our boat chugged out of the little harbor. The sun was setting, and we felt a sadness as we watched her on the shore, her whole being straining toward the unknown vast expanse of water. She knew her calf was out there somewhere.

We returned to the beach the following day. The wind had changed to an off-the-lake direction, and we expected the calf to drift back to the beach. It had, but there were only a few patches of hair left to remind us of the real life drama that had taken place on that mother's day. It is certainly possible that the timber wolf that ate the calf could have been a mother too.

This experience left me with a feeling of awe tinged with some fear. But there are only two natural reasons for a moose to become dangerous to man: during the rutting season when a bull moose might be looking for a fight to impress his chosen mate, and in the early spring when the calves are born. The cow moose who has just become a mother will protect that little fellow with her life if she must. Yet

when that calf is only a few days old she will expect it to keep up with her anywhere, including swimming a good distance in icy water. When the calf hesitates its mother gently but firmly nuzzles her young one into the lake. She swims close to it, making little sounds of encouragement. If it becomes impossible for the calf to go on, he can hitch a ride on his mother's back.

If a moose acts strangely or appears to be dangerous at another time, it is probably a yearling recently driven away by its mother. And, chances are, the yearling is more frightened than the human who thinks he is in danger.

One early spring we had some strange experiences with two yearlings, who were probably twins. They were very curious and mischievous, exhibiting rather unusual behavior for moose. I concluded that since there were two of them, they encouraged each other, and together they were very daring. These two rascals dumped over a box of nets which Ed had spent many hours getting ready to set. Another time they had fun yanking and chewing on a net that was drying on the reels.

The first time I saw them, I thought I was seeing double. Since it was early spring we were living in what we call our little cabin — it only has two rooms — because it is so much easier to heat. While Ed went out on the lake, I decided to stay ashore because it was quite chilly on the lake. I was alone on the island, and I decided to have another cup of coffee before getting started with the housework. The kitchen is small, and it has one fairly large window facing the lake, and directly across from it, another window almost the same size. As I came into the kitchen, I was greeted by a small moose looking in through the lower window. It just stood there as I moved forward into the room. I noticed it was more interested in something across the room than in me. When I came abreast of both windows, I realized what it was. There was the other yearling peering through the upper window. I had a panicky feeling, sort of a claustrophobia of moose. I wondered if I was surrounded by them. I began explaining to the two observers that there was glass separating them. I had a feeling that they might take a notion to walk toward each other, right through the windows. Finally after they made no motion to move on, I turned up the radio real loud. Soon the log walls were throbbing with music. I sneaked a peek at the moose, and they stood there riveted to the spot, ears forward listening intently. They had no intentions of leaving with all that good music to enjoy. So I turned the radio off. They vanished so fast I did not even see in what direction they went. The silence must have scared them.

Last summer was the first time old "Mons" did not come back to his favorite eating place, directly across from our fish house in Hopkins Bay. This old timer had one horn that grew in crooked every year, and this was how we could be sure it was the same bull. After observing him for so many years, we knew his habits pretty well. He walked out into the water to a certain spot every year to feed on the weeds growing on the bottom. We said he was a typical tourist, because he would show up on the first of July and leave on Labor Day. As he grew older he was slower in getting there, and it took him longer to leave. His horns did not polish as fast, but his fur was still black and shiny. He moved much slower near the end, and I am sure the old gent had arthritis. He grumblingly followed a cow, although the old enthusiasm was gone. He even became so disgruntled that he chased us into our cabin. Before he had always politely avoided us. We missed old "Mons" very much.

For quite a few years we'd had a desire to camp for a few days at Lake Siskiwit. But not because we wanted to rough it, as life in our log cabin on Isle Royale was quite primitive, and roughing it was not a treat.

After an involved preparation for the big expedition, we set camp on a little sandy point which formed the east side of a little bay on Lake Siskiwit — a good place to enjoy bathing.

The first day went by too fast. We were starved and almost ate our food right out of the cans. But camping is nothing without a campfire, so we made one beside the water's edge. We had just enough energy to row our old skiff to nearby Eagle Nest Island and back. Returning to camp we sat on the shore and watched the sun go down behind the hills along the north shore of the lake, making an exquisite rainbow of colors reflected on soft white clouds.

This camping trip took place before such luxuries as sleeping bags, air mattresses, gas lanterns and stoves. Our tent was a hand-sewn canvas structure, held in place by wooden poles. We had made beds out of balsam branches, and now we were ready to call it a day. We settled our tired bodies into our lumpy but fresh-smelling beds and prepared for a good night's rest. It was very quiet and a little eerie, and for a short while we missed the security of our homes. The tent looked very fragile. We heard a loon calling in the distance and then there was another sound: branches breaking and much stomping and grunting. That could only be moose.

In our haste to set up camp, we had chosen the flattest spot, which happened to be across a moose trail. Not only did the moose object to our tent being in the way, they discovered that canvas was excellent material to rub the velvet from their horns.

Our tent was pushed back and forth with much exuberance, and we became afraid it would collapse. Our heads were up against the sides of the tent, so we had to sit up most of the night to escape getting them bashed in. Some moose leaped about in the lake snorting and prancing about like horses. This continued until daybreak, then all at once it was very quiet and we exhausted campers fell asleep. The sun was high in the sky when we awakened; it was a beautiful day, and the frightening night was forgotten. Only streaks of velvet on the canvas of our tent were reminders of the night's drama. Our decision to break camp and leave also was forgotten.

We set out to look for an old Indian burial ground which supposedly was located near the sandy point. No luck however, so we explored the woods and beaches and then returned to camp.

The sun was warm and the water sparkled invitingly, so we rowed the old skiff around the shoals and did some trolling. We went further than we intended to, and a brisk wind came up very fast from the southwest. We beached our boat on the lee side of Ryan Island and waited for the wind to die down. We got back to camp just in time to build a fire and cook our favorite böya (stew). Diced bacon and onions are browned in a skillet. To this we added diced potatoes, one can tomatoes, one can corn, one bay leaf and two or three whole allspice. We simmered this for about 20 minutes and just before serving added one can cut up corned beef. It's very good and, quoting my father, "This will stick to the ribs."

Back in the "sack" and completely relaxed, we looked forward to a good night's rest. We talked about the events of the day, but in back of it all was a gnawing suspicion that the moose would be back again as enthusiastic as ever. Dozing off with that thought in mind, I was not at all surprised to awaken and see one side of the tent move a foot or two.

Our camping trip was cut short when Ed hiked the trails to see how we were getting along. It did not take us long to pack up and return home with him.

Our old cabin stands on a rounded knoll, overlooking a beautiful little harbor. A point juts out and almost makes it landlocked. On the end of the point there is an elegant beaver lodge. So far it has been occupied every spring, but I have been dreading the day when I must say to myself "they are gone." Unfortunately the moose and muskrat who also live on this island browse on the same bushes and trees as the beaver. The muskrat steals some of the choice branches from the beavers' stockpile. This conniving little fellow shows his appreciation for the goodies by moving into the lodge and driving out the bugs and lice that make life miserable for the beaver. Apparently the beavers are aware of this favor, because they share their home and their food in exchange for this 'essence of musk.' Although aspen is the preferred food of the beaver, there is little available. So they all must live on the mountain ash and soft maple. The number of beavers has decreased due to the shortage of food, but I am happy that a few remain. Their lodge is very impressive and recently they have changed the shape from single style to a duplex.

We have a marvelous view of the Little Harbor from our kitchen window. It offers a vantage point to watch all the goings on among the wildlife and an excellent chance to observe the beaver. The expression "busy as a beaver" certainly has its basis in reality; it is rare to see the beaver resting on the small beach beside their lodge, basking in the sun. Even then they are scratching their round bellies and plucking lice from their bodies. When they indulge in a gossip session with members of the clan, like monkeys, their interaction includes delousing each other.

When I was a youngster I believed that beavers used their wide flat tails as spatulas for patting and smoothing the mud into place. Of course this is not true, but the tail is an excellent rudder and is used very effectively in communication to sound a warning of danger.

These alarms are often sounded in the middle of the night, loud and clear. We say to ourselves, "Drat that beaver," but we know that many little animals will benefit from that warning.

Beaver lodge across Little Harbor

I was delighted one morning many years ago to see a very wet beaver emerge slowly from the water and waddle up the side of the lodge on its strong hind legs. It looked like a little old man with bad posture. The short front paws were clutching a gob of mud. This mud was pressed against its chest, and when he decided on the exact spot, this very fussy carpenter efficiently plopped the wet mud into place. In time it dries into a cement-like consistency holding the various size sticks in place. There seems to be an engineer in charge of lodge construction and the location of the all-important stockpile. This beaver is generally the largest and probably the oldest member of the family. I've watched this pompous male or female strut around the lodge and deliberately move a stick an inch or two in one direction or the other. Chances are that that stick had been placed there without the proper instructions.

If any person tries helping these industrious animals by placing a stick or two on their lodge, they will find that a beaver will remove it almost at once.

It is possible to tell quite accurately what kind of a fall or winter to expect by observing the beavers' stockpile. If they begin gathering and storing their supply of food early in the season, we can predict an early fall and winter. If the stockpile is extra large, the winter could be long and hard.

We can always tell when there has been an increase in the family. Not from anything as obvious as passing around cigars, but there is a constant parade of goodies, young green sprouts from various desirable bushes, brought home to the beaver kits. The playful little animals love to have fun with (who we assume is) their mother, and she is quite tolerant of their antics.

Once, during a very bad northeaster late one fall, our nearby beavers' stockpile was torn from its mooring and carried away by the wind and current. It was caught by a fallen tree whose arm-like branches grasped it and held it fast. Usually when this happened we did not interfere, because there was enough time before freeze up for them to gather more branches. This time, however, winter was almost upon them, so Ed and I decided to help. It took the good part of an afternoon to tow the heavy pile of branches back to the beaver lodge. The head of the beaver clan watched us closely. He swam ahead of our boat, diving and swimming underwater and coming back to the boat and then heading in the direction of the beaver house. We located the stockpile a little distance from where it had been, a spot we thought better protected. We were told in no uncertain terms by our guide, who showed to us the previous spot, that that was the very best location — and any idiot should know that. So, after hearing several more explosive smacks made by its striking tail, we got the message and moved the stockpile back to his desired location. The chief did not thank us exactly, but I was sure he smiled (Ed said it was a smirk) and began to go about the business of fastening the stockpile by inserting sticks into strategic places.

I think the most amusing incident which I observed near the beaver lodge was a large beaver and one small kit swimming side by side: the big one was towing a good-sized branch with delectable new sprouts growing on it, and the kit, with its tail erect, was proudly towing a single stalk of timothy grass. Unforgettable!

Into this perfect setting entered two troublemakers — a pair of loons. These birds remain mates for life unless one dies, then they will seek another mate.

Loons are beautiful birds probably known best for their eerie calls. They have an unusual repertoire of calls, each one more beautiful than the other. Once in my lifetime I heard a gathering of loons on a moonlit night: one call runs into the other in a continuous symphony of sound.

It is comparable to a chorus of timber wolves when on a full moon night their voices ring out clear and flute-like, an indescribable crescendo of sound, executed for the sheer delight and enjoyment of the participants. You listen in spine-tingling awe and you realize you will never again hear anything compared to this wild exuberance. There is an unearthly

Timber wolf and his reflection in a pond

quality about it, as with their heads raised and pointing toward the full moon, they seem to be tuned into that happy hunting ground in the sky.

My husband and I were fairly sure it was the same pair of loons that came back every spring to the little harbor, because they always returned to the same location to build their nest. Unfortunately this happened to be on the end of the point – the site of the beaver lodge. Loons are extremely awkward on shore because their webbed claws grow so far back, almost under their tail feathers. While they are powerful and fast swimmers, on shore the loons find it necessary to lurch ahead using their wings to propel and balance themselves. Therefore the female cannot be choosy about where to build the nest. She requires a low point of land with some small stones and sticks nearby, and a dropoff, making it possible for her to quietly slip off the nest and submerge out of sight when danger is near. The large eggs left exposed are not apt to be noticed because nature has camouflaged them to blend in with the surroundings.

When we heard an almost continuous loon call coming from the area around the beaver lodge, we knew there was a fight for territory going on — again.

Various loon calls have certain meanings. This particular one could have been a claim to territory or just a plain call for help. At any rate it brought the male to the spot almost at once. The trouble was apparently over the ownership of that piece of land. I found myself rooting for the beaver because I felt they had a priority claim: they spent many years building their home.

The first fight I watched between the loon and the beaver seemed terrible. I expected to see either a dead loon or a vanquished beaver. Oddly enough, though their battle seemed deadly, none of the combatants seemed to be worse off. Loons will not infringe on each other's territory but, evidently to them a beaver lodge was just another pile of mud and sticks. This fight for the right to build a nest on that beaver house went on every spring, and it continued though the nest was established, the eggs laid and the incubation period begun.

Only twice that I remember did the loons successfully hatch their eggs and bring forth young.

Last spring a very odd thing happened to the eggs. The loons left the Little Harbor together, uttering sad and mournful sounds. This usually meant their eggs were destroyed, so Ed and I rowed our skiff across to investigate and found that the beaver had covered the eggs with mud and sticks, breaking them. There had been an exceptionally noisy skirmish earlier that day, and we had seen a beaver sitting on the narrow beach close to the lodge trying to do something about its tail which appeared to have a hole in it. We suspected covering the loons' nest with mud and sticks was just plain getting even.

The snowshoe hare is surprisingly interesting. We never expected to be able to come close to them, but they became used to us. Their numbers increased at an alarming rate; before we realized it, there were snowshoes all over the place. They were all sizes — from little round balls of fur with two large ears and the exaggerated hind feet that resemble snowshoes, to the full grown hare.

At first there seemed to be enough food for them all. A portion of our yard had a good crop of clover, in addition to the dandelions and grass. We realized there was a shortage of food when they started coming out of the woods and walking along the shore, or congregating in the field of buttercups west of the cabin. Soon they were eating the plants down to the roots and our yard looked like it had seen a visitation by locusts. We started feeding them bread and vegetables. They especially liked raisin rye which they ate out of our hands, and would do handsprings for a bit of watermelon.

Toward fall we switched them to cracked corn, since we had more than we needed for the ducks. All the rabbits, even the little ones, adapted to this change in their diet. Ed and I put small piles of corn, quite evenly spaced, along either side of the trail which went past the cabins and into the woods. At first we did not notice that the same ones were stationed in the same places every day until we became familiar with some of their peculiarities: one had lost the hair from its nose during a fight, another one had lighter-colored fur than the others, and yet another had a definite white star on its forehead. One would run up to us and sit on its hind legs to beg for food, and several others had distinguishing characteristics which enabled us to identify them.

We tried to give them their corn at the same time each day, and this was about 7 pm. If we were out late on the lake, we returned to a lineup of hares all along the path. It was as though a top sergeant had given the command, "At your stations." Before ownership of territory was established, there had been considerable arguing and fighting of course. The smaller the rabbit the less chance it had of establishing a position. The larger, older and stronger were at the top of the path.

By sitting quietly within the environs of nature, you can observe some amazing things. On an especially nice warm day I saw a tiny ball of fur emerge from the undergrowth and watched as its mother fed it a small pellet. Investigating later, I discovered it was a dropping of the hares who, oddly enough, seemed to have designated areas (we found two) for the disposal of their droppings. Possibly they did this to guarantee a supply of pellets when they needed them. A naturalist told us that the pellets contain enzymes which are essential for the digestion process of a baby rabbit who is being weaned from its mother's milk. Isn't nature wonderful?

The island we live on is made up mostly of sandstone. We call it red gravel. We noticed oblong scooped-out holes in the trails. Sure enough, they were bathtubs for these interesting little fellows. Actually we became very fond of these trusting, guileless creatures, watching them bathe in their tubs of red dust, rolling around, back and forth, until completely saturated, and then shaking themselves like small puppies, stretching and yawning.

During the peak year for the rabbits, some friends who lived on another island, had a great idea for keeping their grass cut. They wanted to import snowshoe hares, and they did this by paying 25¢ a hare to the children who lived on a neighboring island. Soon they had a real good thing going, never having to swing that heavy old scythe to cut the ever-growing grass. Then one day the investment in their lawn-mower vanished overnight. In its place was a well-fed, very contented fox, lying in the sun, too stuffed to move. So when I hear someone say, "Oh, those dumb rabbits are so prolific." I think, "Sure, they just better be!"

One summer we had a "pet" mink with a very short tail. We called him "Sherlock" because he was always investigating something. He would scamper down the trail pausing along the way to gaze through the open door of the upper cabin, and then walk casually down to the lower cabin, stopping at the door to survey the interior. Then he would proceed to the fish house, and if Ed were dressing fish, he would sit quietly beside him until Ed fed him.

There was also a family of weasels who became very tame. It is hard to imagine weasels being likable. These frisky little animals were very alert, and their shiny black eyes were brightly curious. They were quite playful. They came into our cabin when I was cooking and picked up any crumbs that fell on the floor. All the while they were around us during one summer, they were amazingly honest. I expected them to be little thieves, but really they stole very little food. I believe they trusted us and instinctively knew we would not harm them. We held their food in our hands, and they took it from us very carefully.

Some friends visited with us during the autumn. They were quite startled to hear a soft purring sound coming from the depths of their sleeping bags. Upon investigating they found the weasels had moved into the sleeping bags with them. They knew where to go to keep warm.

These funny little creatures remained friendly until their fur turned white. Their behavior changed with the color of their fur. They became suspicious and wary of us. They no longer came into our cabin begging for food. We wondered if they would have been different if the ground had turned white too. We think they were afraid because instead of blending with the snow, they had turned white before the snow came.

One predator living on Isle Royale is the red fox. His engaging personality gets him a handout wherever he goes.

Our neighbor and friend Sam became so involved in fattening a rather thin-looking fox, he began by feeding a little of this and that. After a few weeks of this and that Sam realized he had a food shortage.

We visited with Sam one day and watched the last piece of ham being eaten very daintily by that adorable fox, who had conned Sam out of the whole thing. The intriguing part was watching this cute little feeder eat right out of your hand and actually lick your fingers without biting your hand.

Another cute trick to watch was how this engaging rascal handled a raw egg. He held it between his front paws while sitting erect. Like all good performers he had perfect timing, and when he had everyone's undivided attention, he lightly tapped the egg on a rock, cracked it and lapped up the contents. This was so interesting and cute to watch, all Sam's eggs went the way of the ham!

A fisherman tries to get out to his nets at dawn. Most of the fishermen's wives on Isle Royale went with their husbands to the nets. I always did because I loved it, awakening to the songs of countless birds.

I think every sweet-singing bird lives on that Island. The most rewarding part of the day is just before the dawn, when the world is waiting for the sunrise. If you listen closely, you will hear a faint tentative song or two like a yawning awareness of the coming day, and then another and another until soon the bird world is awake. Before long there is a throbbing sound of singing.

One summer Ed thought he would see if he could attract the purple martin. He had read about the advantages of having these particular birds around. They are insect eaters, so we would absolutely get rid of every single pesky fly. He built three residences for them, each with four apartments and put them up on poles. He was disappointed to find nary a bird moved into these new houses the first summer. The following summer brought a number of what we thought were female purple martins, but which turned out to be tree swallows. The bird houses were fairly close to our cabin so we could enjoy watching these very busy little birds. At first we thought all the tree swallows that were flitting around were going to nest in all of the twelve apartments. But there was an unusual amount of scolding and fighting for territory, even to destroying one another. Many of the swallows flew low over the water in the bay because they scooped flies right off the water's surface. And this is when the unwary tree swallow can be dive-bombed right out of existence. With tremendous speed his antagonist will hit him with so much force that before he knows it he is lying on the water and is unable to fly again. Perhaps he is knocked unconscious or drowns from too much contact with cold water. It was difficult to believe that with all the available housing only one pair remained.

Every year only one pair of swallows raised one family of young ones. While the male bird was busy fighting off any invaders, the female was doing the work of twelve. She built nests in all of the apartments. We didn't know why she did this. I thought she just plain forgot where she had placed some straws, but these little creatures are too intelligent for that. Our conclusion was that this conniving female intended to convince any prospective tenants that the apartments were already occupied. It did exactly that. We observed strangers coming, and they would look into each house, see the nests and leave. They made no attempts to infringe on the establishment.

This behavior was repeated every year, and it became rather discouraging to us. But last summer a tragedy occurred to our little feathered friends. The female had built her nest, with constant encouragement from her mate, and had laid her eggs, and remained in the house with her eggs except for the times when she went out for food. This day we had been out on the lake in our boat and were in the process of docking it when we noticed a little ball of feathers being carried away across the surface of the water. We were right in assuming that it was an unfortunate tree swallow who had been knocked into the lake. What we did not know then was that it was our own happy little homemaker, who had been chirping about and sitting on the wire with her mate. Several days later we realized there was just one little tree swallow zooming around and sitting on the wires. That was the male. Finally we took the bird house down to check the nest for eggs. There were three of them. We put the house back up on the pole, hoping that we were wrong about the mother. But we were not, and with heart-breaking loyalty her mate returned every day and sat on the wire, looking around anxiously for his mate who did not return.

Among the birds that lived all around us at Wright Island, my favorites beside the tree swallows were the song sparrows. They are such happy inquisitive birds and they give much enjoyment to everyone with their beautiful song. One nosy little fellow saw his image in our bedroom window. He flew at it and pecked the daylights out of what he thought was a competitive male. Finally to put a stop to that continual ratatat racket. I covered the window with window wax. He was happy; he had vanquished the enemy.

All over Menagerie Island there were seagulls nesting among the rocks. I am trying to think of anything as beautiful as a gull. On days when the wind is freshening and the sun is sparkling on the water making it a deeper blue, we watch the gulls swooping down seeking an updraft and finding it. Then zooming gaily aloft soaring and gliding, shafts of white against the sky.

Others remain on the water, bobbing up and down over the waves. Even when they all dive in to feed upon the fish

Our seagull friend, Jonathan

entrails, their rapacious cries are heard by the raven who quickly joins them, their wings flapping and beaks snapping with fish blood splattered all over, and yet they are still beautiful because this is as it should be.

The islands in the outer chain are rookeries for many species of birds. One I find particularly interesting is the blue heron. They stand on the edge of what appears to be a cone-shaped nest, which is perched precariously on the very top branches of the trees. There seems to be one parent on watch at all times until their fledglings are ready to leave the nest and hunt for their own food. They accompany their parents who teach them the art of standing motionless by the edge of a river or lake as a fish swims by. Then one sees why this bird has such a long neck. It can plunge its head into quite deep water and come up with a fish in a flash. In the Siskiwit Bay area there is a swampy place called Mud Lake, and this is the favorite eating place of the herons.

Many different kinds of ducks nest on the islands. My favorite is the female merganser, perhaps because she reminds me of an overworked mother harassed by her younguns. She has an unusually large brood, sometimes as many as twenty cute downy balls will be paddling industriously after her. These are not necessarily all her own ducklings. Somewhere along the way, here and there, she accumulates them from passing entourages. One does not know if the little fellows willfully defect or just become confused and join up without knowing the difference. Of all the female ducks, the merganser seems to be the best mother. She maintains excellent discipline, and she will fight off enemies to the last ditch. When disaster strikes, she has taught the little ducklings to scatter and hide under overhanging bushes.

Unfortunately, being fish eaters, they are the natural enemy of the loon who is also a fish eater. There is no defense against the loon, who will attack the flock from underneath.

Mrs. Merganser, like most of the female ducks, has to raise her own young without the help of her mate. After the mating season he goes on his gay way, wearing his new spring suit of bright colors.

Perhaps the reason I feel empathy for the mother merganser is that at times she looks so frazzled with her top notch awry, perched on her pathetically skinny neck.

The golden eye is an example of the opposite behavior in the method of raising her young. She has no system at all. Her ducklings are adorable, sassy little twerps who soon lose the protection of their mother by darting off in all directions. As a result they are often eaten by the gulls and the loons.

Early one fall two Canadian geese landed at Wright's. They seemed unable to fly and were satisfied to waddle around looking for food. They became very tame, and we fed them cracked corn. Not once would they allow us to forget their corn. If we did, they would come to the kitchen door and complain about it.

One day both of them appeared at the door, and this time their squawking was loud and scolding. Ed guessed that something was wrong and went out to investigate. Sure enough, a very small muskrat was helping himself to their corn. As Ed approached, the little fellow took off in a hurry. The geese remained near the cabin until they were sure it was safe to return, then they strutted importantly and bravely back down the trail to their feeding grounds.

Wright Island is about two miles from the trail that goes to Lake Siskiwit so it's just a short distance by boat and about one half mile by trail from the dock at Malone Bay to the lake. Siskiwit is about seven miles long and dotted with islands. It is also one of the few inland lakes where you can fish for the Mackinaw trout as well as whitefish and very large northern pike.

During the many years we lived on Isle Royale, it was a real treat to go to this lake. The water is just right for swimming and boating and occasionally we trolled, hoping to capture a good-sized trout.

Once while trolling, we thought our lure had caught on a submerged log. We tried to dislodge it, but failed. We wanted to save the lure, so we tried bringing the log to the surface. When it came into view, it was an immense northern pike. It seemed to be as long as our boat, and when it opened its mouth, it looked like a crocodile. If we had brought it into the boat we would have had to get out, so we decided to let it go. Too late, we realized we could have brought it in by towing it to shore, and we probably would be landing a top prize winner. Now, of course, no one believes our fish story!

Returning to live on Isle Royale every summer since I was born has given me many opportunities to share life with God's creatures. It has been my good fortune to know the habits of the beaver, the dignity of the majestic moose, the breathtaking beauty of the gull as the sunlight finds its flashing wings against the azure blue of the sky or the indigo of the water.

To see the sun rise at the eastern end of Hopkins Bay, sometimes a fuzzy misty pink, sometimes an angry red. To watch it set in the west, to see it vanish in a blazing glory of color behind the hills, misty in the distance. And you remember the day that was in between the dawn and dusk. You remember the waves made by the wake of your boat with bubbles churning to the surface and dancing away to make room for more. As you travel east or west you marvel at the changing color of the sky and the beautiful merging of the colors of water with sky until they are as one. You look at the reflected brightness of the white birches as they line the shores, or the shimmering beauty of the quaking aspen. Here and there stands a tall haughty pine, its boughs reaching toward heaven and the deep green forests of spruce and balsam. If you approach softly into shallow water at the end of the bay, you will quite often see moose feeding on weeds that grow on the bottom. The bull lifts his head out of the water, chewing thoughtfully, withdrawn from the mundane. In the summer while his horns are in velvet, he regards you with nearsighted eyes. In the fall when he goes acourting his shyness vanishes. He walks arrogantly about on stiff legs, his horns polished to a bright, shining weapon. As your boat cuts through the water you will notice some ducks along a shore. Two loons will be idling along on the lookout for food. Occasionally you will hear their plaintive calls. You might see a beaver heading for his home, sometimes towing a branch. I get the feeling that a beaver always has a destination; never do I get the feeling that he is just loafing. There is a purpose in everything he does. Rarely does one see an otter, either close to the shore or swimming. They swim faster than beaver and seem loaded with energy. Just once did we see an otter close to our boat — it dove and swam around us, a feisty creature looking for a playmate. They are sleek beauties.

Now you pass a tract of land on the north side of Siskiwit Bay that once was the townsite of the Island Mine. It is hard to imagine that this area had at one time been settled by miners and their families. There was a large dock to accommodate the schooners and a warehouse which eventually burned. Strangely enough there is absolutely nothing left of that bustling village. However, as you walk the trail that takes you up into the Sugar Mountain area, and across the Red Oak Ridge and on to join the Greenstone Ridge Trail, you may hear the lilting song of the Irish or Welsh miner, echoing back over the many years as he walked this same trail to the Island Mine location. In fact as you pass that way you can see a part of the machinery used and the dross of slag standing in piles, a reminder of the past. Not only do these slag piles help us to know about the history of the Island, they provide excellent places for the water snakes to bask in the sun.

You continue on to the end of the bay and run your boat ashore to have a cup of coffee and sandwiches. This area is rich in history also. Senter Point which divides this end of Siskiwit Bay into two has the remains of a stone powder house used by the Island Mine in the 1870's.

Our main reason for stopping on this beach for lunch, however, is to lazily move some of the beach stones and look for the purple or blue agate and the ruby red carnelians.

This is a typical summer day, invigorating in spite of the hot sun, with a brisk breeze making ripples on the water. Now we head our boat toward home, and as we come into the bay, and, as usual, pass the same point of chiseled red rock with the mountain ash, evergreens and birches growing there, we feast our eyes on all this splendor and pray silently "Thank you, oh Lord."

There is hope in our hearts that this land will remain clean and alive and eternal, a home for the God-given wild creatures large and small that roam this land. May the unpolluted air be filled with the song of birds. As we seem to glide over the water idly watching a gull in flight, or a merganser hen hurrying her brood toward the shore, we feel the gentle blessings from heaven, the soothing balminess of nature. It is great to be alive.

APPENDIX

If the new moon can hold water, then to rain it hadn't otter. If the new moon is tipped a lot, then much rain is what we got.

Evening red and morning grey is the beginning of a pretty fair day. Evening grey and morning red, sailor you can stay in bed.

Rain before seven; through before eleven.

A northeast blow will bring rain or snow.

Look at the new moon over your left shoulder, lucky you, your wish will come true.

Sunset bright is a sailor's delight.

A full moon will cast its spell, be calm like the weather, my dear Nell.

There is a storm beginning to form if the current rushes in and out. So batten the hatches and fasten the latches, your sails must wait, forlorn.

A moon ringer, will bring a humdinger.

THE LEGEND OF CEMETERY ISLAND

I walked into the dark, damp woods of this rather ordinary-looking island. I saw the same kind of trees, the same kind of bushes and the same kind of grass as all the other islands had. And the beach looked the same. But that is where the similarity ended. This was "Cemetery Island" — a place that made you want to speak softly and walk gently. It was a quiet place, and my imagination was working. At last I was going to be able to find out why this particular island was so bathed in mystery. Whenever I asked anyone about the graves and how they were marked and if the dead had been copper miners or lumberjacks and did they die from an epidemic, the answers were always evasive and noncommittal.

When I was in my early 20's and we were visiting some friends at Caribou Island, I decided to row over to Cemetery Island, which was real close by, and look for those graves. No one wanted to accompany me.

There were no trails to follow, and I got the feeling that no one, at any time, had walked around on that island. But this must not be so, because I had been told that once a year a wreath was placed on the graves by some official, usually an employee of the park service.

A strange stillness seemed to be waiting for anyone who dared to venture therein. It occurred to me that I would cut my expedition very short, and instead of walking around the little island, I would first walk toward the center.

The underbrush was very thick as was the crown of foliage from the trees that covered the island. Nowhere did the sun shine through. I had an eerie feeling. There was not a sound of squirrel or a rabbit hopping around or the song of a bird. Just nothing but the beating of my heart.

Strange how easy it is to blow every little thing out of proportion. It would not have surprised me in the least if I had been joined by a ghost of the past. I had an urge to turn and run, but just then I discovered that I was almost standing on a grave.

This was indeed a completely uncared for cemetery. There were just a few scattered wooden crosses made by nailing two pieces of wood together, and they were leaning at crazy angles. I think some names had been written on them, or so I was told, but they were gone now. Time and weather had obliterated them. No identity. I felt a sadness for those who were left in isolation and uncared for in a strange land.

Reality was back, and I made tracks, very positive ones, back to my boat. I untied the landing rope and pushed away from shore at once. I rowed away as fast as possible as if I were being pursued. And by what? My imagination.

The rumor that seems to be accepted most often is that a load of liquor was brought to a nearby mining town, near Ransom Mine, where Daisy Farm Campground is now. There was an unbelievable brawl. Pent-up emotions surfaced and hatred among a few was so strong, it became a fight to the finish. I am told there were no women or children buried there, so that may be true.

[Ingeborg Holte wrote this short piece as an assignment for a Writers' Class in the fall of 1983, ten years after she wrote the major manuscript.
— Ed.]